Man Up Volume 2:
VIPER

A Winner's Code

Edet Martin

This publication provides accurate information on the subject matter but does not constitute legal, investment, accounting, or professional advice. While the author and publisher have made their best efforts, they disclaim any warranties regarding the book's accuracy or fitness for a particular purpose. Consult a professional for advice specific to your situation. The author and publisher are not liable for any damages, including but not limited to financial, incidental, or consequential losses.

ISBN (Paperback): 979-8-234-09198-7

Book Cover by Edet Martin

Published by Legacy Literary House

www.legacyliteraryhouse.com

First Edition 2026

Introduction: The Moment a Man Decides

• • • •

Most men don't fail because they're weak. They fail because they're wandering.

The VIPER Mindset

• • • •

A VIPER man moves with intention: clear vision, consistent effort, and structured planning.

Table of Contents

Introduction
Why VIPER?

Every generation of men faces a decision: drift with the current of life or take command of their destiny. Too many choose to drift. They live reactive lives, ruled by circumstances, rather than proactive lives, guided by vision. This book is for the men who are done drifting.

When I wrote Man Up (Volume 1), it was a call for young men to take responsibility for their choices, their discipline, and their lives. The response was powerful. Men wrote to me, saying the book was the wake-up call they needed. But many also asked: What's next? How do you not just "man up," but actually build a life worth living?

That's why this book exists. Man Up, Volume 2: VIPER: A Winner's Code isn't about hype, theory, or motivational fluff. It's about a code, a way of living, a set of principles that transforms ordinary men into focused, disciplined, and resilient individuals.

I chose the word Viper for a reason. A viper is not a creature you take lightly. You don't approach it casually, and you don't underestimate it. You respect it because of what it represents: danger, precision, and focus. A man who follows the VIPER code, Vision, Inspiration, Plan, Effort, Resilience, is the same. He is not here to play games. He is on a mission. Every action is deliberate. Every step moves him toward victory.

This book isn't meant to be read passively. It's meant to challenge you, confront you, and ultimately build you. Each chapter will not only tell a story and share lessons but also push you to act. Because knowledge without application is wasted.

The world doesn't need more men who just talk. It needs more men who do. And by the time you finish this book, you'll have the tools, stories, and strategies to not only man up, but to rise up.

Again, why VIPER? Because a viper is fast, precise, and intentional. It doesn't waste energy. It doesn't strike unless it has a purpose. A viper survives and thrives because it moves with clarity and confidence. That's how you need to move in life.

In a world brimming with challenges and opportunities, the difference between those who succeed and those who falter often lies in a simple yet powerful framework. Too many men live without direction. They chase distractions, copy other people's paths, or let life push them around. That's not you. You're here because you want more. You want to stand out, to build something real, to live with impact.

I coined the acronym VIPER, which stands for Vision, Inspiration, Plan, Effort, and Resilience. This code encapsulates the essential elements needed to turn dreams into reality.

The VIPER code gives you the tools to do exactly that:

- Vision: Knowing where you're going.

- Inspiration: Fueling your fire every day.

- Plan: Structuring your steps so success isn't left to chance.

- Effort: Doing the hard work, even when it isn't glamorous.

- Resilience: Rising every time you fall, stronger and smarter than before.

These five principles are not theory. They're practical. They're real. And if you commit to them, they will change the way you move in the world.

This book isn't long because I don't believe in wasting words. It's short, sharp, and direct, like a viper's strike. Take these lessons seriously, apply them daily, and watch your life transform.

Two Men, One Code

To make this real, I'm not giving you random stories. Instead, you'll follow two men through these pages:

Khari, 18 years old, standing at the starting line of manhood.

Lewis, 41 years old, standing at a crossroads, deciding whether to coast or build his second half.

Khari represents the young man trying to create a future before the world defines it for him.

Lewis represents the seasoned man, realizing it's not too late to rewrite his story and leave a legacy.

How to Read This Book

Don't read this book passively. Use it like a manual. At the end of each chapter, you'll find reflection questions and action steps. Do them. Write them out. Test them. By the end, you won't just know the VIPER Code, you'll live it.

Final Word

The world needs more men who move with vision, fire, structure, grit, and resilience. Men who strike with precision. That's what this book is here to build.

Let's get to work.

Dedication

• • • •

To my father and brothers, the men who have shaped me in ways words can barely capture.

You taught me that strength is more than muscle; it's discipline, courage, and the willingness to stand when others sit. You showed me that leadership isn't just about giving orders, but about living as an example worth following. Your sacrifices and unshakable will have been the standards I measure myself against.

Every lesson you lived, I carry with me, and every victory I earn is built on the foundation you laid. Thank you for being strong examples of what it means to be a man. Each of you has inspired me to push harder, stand taller, and never shrink back from life's battles.

Your example reminds me that greatness is built not on words, but on action, discipline, and resilience. This book is for you, the men who live the code every day.

To every man who sees himself in Khari or Lewis, whether you're just starting out or rebuilding in midlife, this book is for you. May you carry this code and live it daily.

Acknowledgment

• • • •

I want to honor the men who inspired me through their words, struggles, victories, and even their quiet examples. Some guided me directly; others simply lived in a way that pushed me to be better. You reminded me that manhood is not about drifting, it's about vision, grit, and legacy.

To Clinton Armstrong, William Brimage, Eric Crawford, Gary Davis, Dexter Drakeford, John Dunbar, Jon Dunbar, Charles Ellis, David Ford, Edward Hall, Demetrice Hall, Willie Hall, Roy Holman, Peter King, Dr. Jason Leary, Johnny Martin, Willie Martin, Anthony Martin, Curtis Mathis, Willie Mathis, Mario Maitland, Brad Mullins, Robert Oliver, Aaron Parker, Robert Rhodes, Antonio Rhodes, Brandon Roberts, Brant Roberts, John Roberts, Chris Simms, Calvin Smith, Terrance Singleton, James Overstreet, and Johnny Watson. Each one of you has inspired me in some form or fashion. You may not have even known it, but through your lives, your words, your struggles, and your victories, you have left an imprint that continues to push me forward.

Your lives have shown me what discipline looks like, what resilience feels like, and what true leadership requires. Some of you have guided me directly; others through quiet example; and many simply by the way you live each day. Whether through family, friendship, brotherhood, or mentorship, you have each stood as a reminder that men can be strong yet humble, bold yet wise, and committed to something greater than themselves.

I thank you all for being pillars of inspiration, for lighting the path forward, and for proving that greatness is built through consistency, faith, and courage. You are more than just men I know, you are men I honor.

Chapter 1
Vision
The Blueprint of Success

• • • •

Vision is the ability to see beyond where you are today and to picture where you're going tomorrow. Without it, men drift. With it, men move with purpose.

Vision is the ability to see beyond your present reality and into the future you want to create. It's the mental picture of the man you're becoming and the life you're building. Vision gives your life direction, focus, and meaning. Without it, you're just reacting to whatever happens. With it, you move with purpose.

A man without vision is like a ship without a compass, he moves, but he goes nowhere. He drifts with the waves, controlled by the wind, at the mercy of the storm. That's how too many young men live today: moving, but not progressing; busy, but not building.

A clear vision motivates you to push through challenges and gives meaning to the grind. It also builds resilience. When setbacks hit, your vision reminds you why you started and why quitting isn't an option. For teams, vision brings alignment and unity; for individuals, it clarifies identity and purpose.

Vision is also a filter for decisions. When opportunities arise, you can measure them against your vision and choose the ones that move you closer to your goal. Most importantly, vision fuels innovation and growth. It pushes you to think bigger, explore possibilities, and become the man you set out to be.

Visualization tools, like vision boards or guided imagery, can make your goals feel real before you achieve them. Athletes, leaders, and high performers use these techniques because the brain responds to imagined success much like it does to real experience. Creating a vision board or practicing guided imagery daily keeps your goals at the front of your mind and reinforces your commitment. When paired with discipline, vision becomes more than an idea. It becomes a roadmap.

• • • •

Khari's Vision

Khari was eighteen, standing in the middle of his graduation crowd with his cap tilted and his diploma rolled in his hand. Around him, classmates celebrated. Some heading to college, some straight to jobs, others still undecided.

But Khari felt something different. Instead of excitement, he felt a knot in his stomach. He didn't know what came next. No college acceptance letter in his pocket. No job lined up. Just a diploma and questions.

That night, he sat on the edge of his bed, staring at his cracked phone screen, scrolling through social media and comparing himself to classmates posting about scholarships, moving into dorms, or joining the military. For a moment, he felt behind before life had even started.

Then his grandmother walked in. She set an old shoebox on his lap. Inside were family photos of his mother working long shifts, his uncles who had struggled with jail and dead-end jobs, cousins who hadn't made it past high school.

His grandmother looked him in the eye and said, "You don't have to repeat this. But if you don't know where you're going, life will choose for you."

That hit him deep. For the first time, Khari realized his life didn't have to be a repeat of the past, but it also wouldn't change by accident. He lay back on his bed, eyes open in the dark, picturing the man he wanted to become. He saw himself waking up early, lacing up his boots, and heading to work as an electrician; strong, confident, focused. He imagined walking into his own apartment—clean, organized, peaceful—with a photo of his grandmother smiling from the kitchen counter. He could see his first car parked outside, one he bought outright, no co-signer. He saw himself calm, disciplined, and proud, and it felt real enough to touch.

That night, he grabbed a spiral notebook and wrote his first Five-Year Vision Map. He didn't have every answer, but he had direction:

- Enrolling in trade school for electrical work.
- Saving enough to move into his own apartment.
- Buying his first car outright, no co-signer.
- Staying in shape, strong and disciplined.
- Supporting his grandmother, making her proud.

It wasn't polished, but it was a map, his first blueprint for manhood. For Khari, vision became the compass that kept him from drifting into the same cycle he saw around him.

• • • •

Lewis's Vision

Lewis was forty-one, sitting in his car outside the office, gripping the steering wheel after another long day. He had the kind of life people would call "stable". A steady job, a house, a wife, and two kids. But deep down, he knew the truth: he had been drifting for years. He worked hard, but not with direction. His career had plateaued. His health was slipping, thirty extra pounds around his waist, blood pressure medicine lined up on the counter. His marriage was steady but distant. His kids were growing up fast, and he realized he was missing the chance to leave them more than just bills and stories about "how hard he worked."

That night, after everyone went to bed, Lewis sat at the kitchen table with a blank journal. He asked himself the hardest question: "What do I want the second half of my life to look like?"

He closed his eyes and, for the first time in a long time, allowed himself to see it. He pictured himself coming home from work—not drained but fulfilled. His kids running up to him, shouting, "Dad!" He saw his wife smiling again, the spark back in her eyes. He saw himself jogging in the morning, lighter, stronger, no more pills on the counter. He imagined walking his daughter down the aisle one day. Confident, proud, and healthy. He saw a man leading from the front, not just at work, but at home and in his community.

When he opened his eyes, clarity replaced the fog. He began to write, not just tasks, but a new direction:

For the first time in years, he wrote not a to-do list, but a vision map:

- Be present with his kids before they are gone: family dinners, real conversations, coaching their sports teams.
- Drop 25 pounds, get back into the shape he was in at 25, so he could keep up with his kids.
- Build financial stability, set up a college fund, invest smart, leave assets, not debts.
- Rekindle his marriage with effort and intentionality.
- Lead not just at work, but in his home and community.

As he finished writing, he felt something he hadn't felt in years: clarity. His vision wasn't about starting over, it was about building forward.

• • • •

Why Vision Matters

For Khari, vision meant escaping a cycle before it trapped him.

For Lewis, vision meant rewriting his second half before it was too late.

Vision is the starting point of every great achievement. Without it, you're drifting. With it, you're dangerous. A clear vision does six things for a man:

- Gives Direction: Without vision, you're walking in circles. With vision, every step has a purpose.
- Creates Motivation: You're not just grinding; you're grinding for something.
- Builds Resilience: When life hits you, vision reminds you why you can't quit.
- Sharpens Decisions: Every choice becomes simple: does it move me closer to my vision, or farther away?
- Demands Discipline: Vision makes sacrifice worth it because you see where you're going.
- Commands Respect: Men with vision carry themselves differently. Others notice it.

Think of vision as the blueprint for your life. No builder starts a house without a plan. No soldier steps into battle without a mission. And no man should move through life without knowing where he's headed.

• • • •

5 Common Vision Killers

- Distractions – Wasting hours on social media, partying, or chasing empty thrills.
- Peer Pressure – Following the crowd instead of leading yourself.
- Fear – Doubting yourself before you even start.
- Lack of Clarity – Not writing down exactly what you want.
- Comfort Zone – Settling for "good enough" instead of pushing for better.

Vision-Building Exercise: Your 5-Year Life Map
Take 20 minutes and answer the following:

- Where do you see yourself in 5 years?
- What kind of man do you want to be?

- What career or financial situation do you want?
- What relationships do you want with family, friends, or a partner?
- What habits or skills will you need to get there?
- Write it down—this is your starting vision.

Reflection Questions

- Where am I drifting in life right now?
- What would my life look like in five years if I refused to quit?
- What picture do I want my kids, family, or future self to see when they look at me?

Key Takeaways

- Vision is the blueprint of your life. Without it, you drift.
- Writing down your vision gives you direction when you feel lost.
- Kill distractions, peer pressure, and fear.
- Your five-year life map is the first step toward becoming the man you want to be.

Action Step

Take out a notebook. Write down what your life looks like five years from now if you refuse to quit. Be specific: career, money, health, relationships, faith, impact. Don't just write what sounds good; write what you truly want. This is the first draft of your vision.

Keep it with you. Read it often. Let it burn into your mind until it drives you forward.

Because without a vision, you'll live someone else's story. With a vision, you'll write your own.

Chapter 2
Inspiration
Fueling Your Journey

• • • •

Inspiration is the spark that ignites the fire of ambition. It can come from many sources: personal experiences, influential figures, or even nature.

Motivation fades; inspiration lasts. Motivation is about mood, how you feel in the moment. Inspiration is about meaning, why you keep moving when you don't feel like it.

Inspiration is the spark that keeps your vision alive. It's the fire inside you that pushes you to keep going when the road gets hard. If vision shows you where you're headed, inspiration gives you the energy to walk the path.

Motivation fades; inspiration lasts. Motivation depends on how you feel in the moment. Inspiration comes from something deeper, your values, your role models, your calling, your desire to leave a mark.

The journey toward your vision will get tough. There will be days when you don't feel like grinding, when you question yourself, when setbacks make you want to quit. That's when inspiration matters most. It reminds you why you started in the first place.

When you're inspired, you move with energy and passion—and that passion builds commitment. Inspiration also gives you purpose. It helps you connect with your "why," the deeper reason behind the work. This sense of purpose keeps you grounded when obstacles arise.

Inspiration is contagious too. When you're inspired, those around you feed off that energy, creating stronger relationships and teamwork.

The best way to keep your inspiration alive is by knowing your sources of motivation. For some, it's family. For others, it's faith, mentors, or a desire to leave a legacy. The key is to identify what truly drives you, then feed it daily. Create an environment that supports inspiration: spend time with people who lift you, engage in activities that spark creativity, and surround yourself with reminders of your purpose. Unlike short bursts of hype, real inspiration builds a mindset that sustains motivation for the long haul.

• • • •

Khari's Spark

Khari was two months out of high school, working part-time at a fast-food spot to help with bills at home. Most of his friends were either off at college or drifting around, partying every weekend.

One evening, he came home late and found his younger sister sitting at the kitchen table doing homework. She looked up and said, "Khari, when I grow up, I want to do what you do."

At first, he laughed it off. But later that night, lying in bed, those words replayed in his head. His sister wasn't talking about fast food or late nights—she was saying she saw him as her example. That realization hit him hard: she's watching me. If he gave up, she would think giving up was normal. If he drifted, she'd think drifting was okay.

The next morning, Khari taped a note to his mirror: "She's watching. Don't quit." That single moment became his fuel. Whenever he felt tired at work or doubted his plan, he thought of his sister. Her words lit his fire when motivation ran out.

• • • •

Lewis's Fire

Lewis had spent years running on autopilot—work, bills, routine. He loved his kids, but he knew he wasn't giving them his best.

One Saturday afternoon, his 12-year-old son asked if he'd come outside and throw the football around. Lewis agreed, but after ten minutes, his chest burned and his legs felt heavy. Embarrassed, he bent over, hands on his knees, while his son stood waiting with the ball.

His son looked at him and asked, "Dad, are you okay?" Lewis nodded, but inside...

Shame hit like a punch. Lewis realized that if he couldn't even play ball with his son, how could he lead him into manhood? That night, he sat on the edge of his bed, replaying the moment. He thought of his kids looking to him not just for money or a roof, but for example. He didn't want them to remember a father who was too tired, too heavy, or too distracted. He wanted them to see a man who showed up with strength, presence, and energy. That became his why. From then on, every workout, every healthier meal, every late night he chose discipline over comfort—he wasn't doing it for himself alone. He was doing it for the two sets of eyes watching his every move.

Teaching: Why Inspiration Matters

Inspiration is more than a good feeling, it's the fuel that keeps men pushing forward. Without it, discipline feels like drudgery. With it, every challenge feels worth it. Inspiration is what turns ordinary effort into extraordinary achievement.

Here's what inspiration does for you:

Ignites Motivation – It's the push to take the first step when you'd rather stay still.

Enhances Creativity – Inspiration opens your mind to new ways of solving problems.

Builds Resilience – When you're inspired, setbacks don't crush you; they challenge you.

Drives Passion – Inspired men don't just work; they work with fire in their chest.

Connects You to Purpose – Inspiration reminds you why you started and why you can't quit.

• • • •

Practical Applications of Inspiration

- Look Back to Look Forward – Reflect on what used to inspire you: childhood passions, past mentors, or moments when you felt most alive. Often, the seeds of your purpose were planted long ago.
- Fuel Up Daily – Don't wait for inspiration to show up. Seek it. Read books, listen to podcasts, surround yourself with driven people, and consume content that fuels growth.
- Create Inspiring Environments – Your surroundings matter. Keep a workspace, playlist, or routine that sparks energy in you.
- Stay Close to Role Models – Inspiration is contagious. Spend time with men who challenge you to level up.

Turn Inspiration into Action – Don't stop at feeling fired up, channel that energy into your plan.

Sources of Inspiration

- Faith – Believing life has a higher purpose.
- Family – Providing for and protecting those you love.
- Mentors – Following someone who's been where you want to go.
- Legacy – Considering what people will say about you.
- Responsibility – Realizing people depend on you.

Inspiration Pitfalls

- Social Media Hype – Chasing trends instead of building real goals.

- Shallow Motivation – Seeking quick fixes with no lasting meaning.
- Comparison – Trying to copy someone else's life instead of creating your own.

Daily Inspiration Habits

- Morning Routine – Center yourself before the world distracts you.
- Mentor Check-Ins – Surround yourself with people who challenge you.
- Affirmations – Remind yourself of your vision.
- Reading or Listening – Consume content that lifts you higher.
- Accountability Partner – Someone who will call you out and keep you on track.

Reflection Questions

- Who or what truly inspires me to be better?
- Am I chasing hype or building something lasting?
- What would I fight for every morning?

Key Takeaways

- Inspiration keeps your vision alive.
- Your "why" must be stronger than your excuses.
- Build daily habits that keep your fire lit.

Action Step

Write down three things that inspire you deeply. One should be personal (like Khari's sister), one relational (like Lewis's kids), and one bigger than yourself (faith, purpose, legacy).

Post that list somewhere you'll see it daily. When fatigue or doubt shows up, revisit it.

Because when vision gives you the target, inspiration gives you the fire to hit it.

Chapter 3
Plan
Mapping the Path to Success

• • • •

Vision shows you where you want to go. Inspiration fuels you to get moving. But without a plan, you're walking in circles.

A plan is the bridge between dreams and reality. It turns "someday" into "step one."

A plan is the bridge between your vision and your reality. It turns dreams into steps, and steps into progress. Without a plan, vision remains just a picture in your head. With a plan, vision becomes a roadmap you can follow every single day.

Please understand: a dream without a plan is just a wish. That's why most people never reach their goals—they talk big, but they never break it down into action. They expect life to hand them success, when success only comes to those who structure their grind.

A strong plan provides focus, clarifies priorities, and keeps you accountable. It guides decision-making by showing which choices align with your goals. A plan also helps anticipate challenges. By thinking ahead, you're better prepared to adjust when life throws curveballs. With milestones built in, a plan allows you to track progress and celebrate wins along the way.

Effective planning starts with goal setting. The most successful goals are SMART: specific, measurable, achievable, relevant, and time-bound. Once goals are clear, prioritization determines what comes first and what can wait. Tools like the Eisenhower Matrix help you separate urgent tasks from important ones, keeping you focused on what truly matters.

Planning also builds confidence. When you know your next step, you walk into challenges with clarity instead of confusion. At the end of the day, planning is about turning vision into structured action.

Here's the truth: life rewards strategy, not luck. Talent might open a door, but planning keeps you in the room.

• • • •

Khari's First Roadmap

After sketching his five-year vision, Khari realized something: the picture was clear, but the path was blurry. He knew what he wanted—trade school, a car, his own place—but he had no idea how to get there.

For a while, he drifted. He worked fast-food shifts, came home tired, and told himself, "One day I'll figure it out." But "one day" never comes unless you map it out. One Sunday, his grandmother asked him to sit with her at the kitchen table. She slid a blank sheet of paper across and said, "Write down the first three steps you can take toward your vision. Not the big picture, the first three."

Khari wrote slowly:

Apply for financial aid at the local trade school.

Save $1,000 for a used car.

Pick up one extra shift per week.

It wasn't complicated, but it was a start. The first week, he applied for school. He didn't hear back right away, and doubt crept in. But the plan reminded him what to do next. He saved every extra dollar instead of wasting it. Within four months, he bought a used car. By the fall, he was...

Khari enrolled in night classes for electrical work. His vision had given him direction. His plan gave him steps. And each small win—the car, the enrollment—proved the plan was working.

• • • •

Lewis's Second-Half Blueprint

At 41, Lewis's vision was clear: drop weight, strengthen his family ties, and build financial stability. But, just like Khari, he realized the picture wasn't enough. Without a plan, his vision was just talk.

For years, Lewis had set vague goals: "I'll lose weight," "I'll spend more time with my kids," "I'll save more money." But without structure, nothing stuck. This time, he did it differently. He broke his goals into specific milestones:

Health: Walk 30 minutes five times a week, cut soda, lose 5 pounds in the first month.

Family: Block out two evenings a week for dinner and one Saturday morning for activities with the kids—non-negotiable.

Finances: Open a college savings account, set up automatic deposits, and cut $200 of unnecessary expenses each month.

The plan didn't erase the grind. Some weeks, he skipped workouts. Some months, money was tighter than expected. But the structure kept him honest. Instead of quitting, he adjusted. Six months later, he was down 15 pounds, his kids were used to family nights, and his savings account had its first real balance.

The results weren't dramatic, but they were real. Lewis learned what Khari was learning too: the man with a plan builds. The man without one drifts.

• • • •

Why a Plan Matters

Dreams are cheap. A plan is priceless. Many men fail not because they lack desire, but because they lack direction. A plan bridges the gap between vision and victory.

Here's what a strong plan gives you:

- Direction – It transforms vague goals into clear, actionable steps.

- Accountability – A plan keeps you honest about what you said you'd do.
- Resource Control – It forces you to use your time, money, and energy wisely.
- Progress Tracking – It lets you measure how far you've come and how far you need to go.
- Adaptability – Plans can change, but having one gives you something to adjust instead of starting from nothing.

Practical Applications of Planning

- Use the SMART Method – Make goals Specific, Measurable, Achievable, Relevant, and Time-bound. For example, "I want to save money" becomes "I will save $5,000 by December 31st."
- Break Big Goals into Small Wins – Think in terms of daily or weekly targets instead of overwhelming yourself with the end result.
- Write It Down – Plans in your head get forgotten. Plans on paper get executed.
- Schedule It – Put your plan on a calendar. If it's not scheduled, it doesn't exist.
- Review and Adjust – Check your plan weekly. Celebrate progress, correct mistakes, and keep moving.

The Big Vision → Milestones → Daily Steps Formula

- Big Vision – 5–10-year goal
- Milestones – Checkpoints (Year 1, 3, 5)
- Daily Steps – Habits to reach milestones

Common Planning Mistakes

- Overplanning without acting

- Waiting for the "perfect time"
- Setting vague goals
- Letting fear keep you from step one

90-Day Success Plan Worksheet

- Define one major goal
- Break it into three milestones
- Set weekly action steps
- Review weekly

Reflection Questions

- What goal have I been avoiding?
- What stops me from breaking it down into steps?
- What action can I take tonight?

Key Takeaways

- A plan turns vision into action.
- Break goals into milestones and daily steps.
- Start now and adjust as you go.

Action Step
Write a 90-day personal success plan:

- Choose one area of your life (career, health, money, or relationships).
- Define a clear goal for the next three months.
- Break it into weekly steps.
- Write down three daily habits that support this goal.

Because vision gives you the picture, planning gives you the bridge.

Chapter 4
Effort
The Engine of Achievement

••••

Effort is the driving force that propels you toward your goals. It is about taking consistent action and pushing through obstacles.

Vision shows you the destination. Inspiration gives you the fire. A plan lays out the steps.

But none of it matters if you don't do the work.

Effort is the price of success.

It's the grind, the reps, the routines, the sacrifices that separate men who dream from men who build.

Effort is the price of success. Vision sets the target, inspiration fuels the fire, and planning draws the map—but none of it matters if you don't put in the work. Too many men want the reward without the grind. They want the results without the sacrifice. But life doesn't work that way. You don't get what you want. You get what you work for. Effort is what separates talkers from doers. It's the difference between a man who dreams about success and a man who achieves it.

Talent will open the door, but effort keeps you in the room. Effort is the consistent work you put in, day after day, to achieve your goals. Unlike talent, effort is always under your control. It builds skill, sharpens resilience, and fuels personal growth. Every rep in the gym, every late night of study, every extra mile on the road—these small deposits of effort compound into mastery over time.

Effort requires discipline and hard work. Discipline builds structure and consistency; hard work drives momentum and progress. Together, they create grit—the refusal to quit when things get tough. A strong work ethic means showing up, avoiding procrastination, and pushing past the urge for comfort. Strategies like creating routines, breaking big goals into smaller steps, and managing time effectively make effort sustainable. Effort is not glamorous, but it is non-negotiable. In the end, it's not the man with the most talent who wins—it's the man willing to give the most effort.

• • • •

Khari's Grind

Trade school classes had started, and Khari quickly realized it wasn't going to be easy. The first week, he came home drained—eight hours at work flipping burgers, then three hours of evening classes, and homework waiting on his desk. By the second week, he wanted to quit. His friends texted him about parties. Some laughed, saying, "Man, why are you working so hard? You're only 18. Live your life."

But Khari remembered his plan. He remembered his sister watching. So he showed up anyway. Every night, he forced himself to stay awake one extra hour to review notes. Every weekend, while friends slept in, he worked double shifts to save for the tools he would need when he finished school. It wasn't glamorous. Nobody applauded. But slowly, things changed. His grades stayed solid. His bank account grew. His body adjusted to the grind.

Khari learned something most men don't realize until later: consistency beats talent. He wasn't the smartest in class, but he was the most consistent. And consistency is effort's greatest weapon.

• • • •

Lewis's Discipline

Lewis's plan looked good on paper—workouts, family time, financial goals—but effort made it real. The first Monday of his new routine, he woke at 5:30 a.m. to walk. His alarm rang, and the old Lewis wanted to roll over. But he forced his feet to the floor. That was effort.

When his coworkers ordered pizza at lunch, Lewis opened his container of grilled chicken and vegetables. That was effort.

When his kids asked to play after work, even though he was tired, he said yes. That was effort.

Week after week, these small deposits of effort added up. He dropped weight. He had more energy. His kids noticed the difference. His wife noticed the difference. It wasn't about one dramatic moment—it was about showing up, over and over, until effort became habit. Lewis learned that your effort writes your reputation. His kids no longer saw a dad who was always too tired; they saw a man who pushed himself and still showed up for them.

Why Effort Wins

Effort is the multiplier. It makes average men dangerous. Too many men rely on talent or potential, but talent without effort is wasted. Effort is the force multiplier—it takes whatever gifts you have and pushes them to their full potential.

Here's what effort does:

- Builds Consistency – Showing up day after day creates momentum.
- Beats Talent – Over time, hard work outpaces raw skill.
- Strengthens Discipline – Effort builds habits that make you dependable.
- Reveals Character – A man's effort shows what he truly values.
- Creates Opportunity – The harder you work, the "luckier" you seem to get.

Practical Applications of Effort

- Outwork Yesterday – Don't compete against others; compete against who you were yesterday.
- Consistency Over Intensity – A little effort every day beats a huge effort once in a while.
- Use Systems – Build daily routines that make effort automatic (morning workouts, nightly reading, weekly reviews).
- Track Effort, Not Just Results – Results take time, but effort is in your control today.
- Find Fuel – Effort is easier when it's tied to your vision and inspiration.

Daily Effort Rituals

- Set three non-negotiables every day
- Control your morning
- Work in focused blocks
- Sacrifice temporary comfort
- Consistency over intensity

Chapter 4: Effort
30-Day Effort Challenge

- Write down three non-negotiables.
- Do them daily.
- Track your progress on a calendar.
- Review your progress after 30 days.

Reflection Questions

- Where in my life am I giving minimum effort but expecting maximum results?
- Where am I making excuses?

- What area could I give more?
- How would my life change if I gave consistent effort for six months?

Key Takeaways

- Effort beats talent when talent won't work.
- Consistency matters more than perfection.
- Avoid excuses, comfort, and impatience.

Action Step

Take one goal from your 90-Day Plan. Write down three daily actions you will commit to—no excuses. Do them for 30 days. Track them. Adjust them. But don't skip them.

Because success isn't handed out. It's earned. And the payment is effort.

Chapter 5
Resilience
Bouncing Back from Setbacks

• • • •

Vision sets your direction. Inspiration fuels your fire. Planning maps the steps. Effort pushes you forward.

But resilience determines whether you finish or fold.

Every man gets knocked down. Resilience is the decision to rise again.

Resilience is your ability to rise after every fall. It's what separates men who finish from men who quit. Life will knock you down—friends, family, work, health, setbacks—it doesn't matter. What matters is whether you get back up.

Most men fail not because they lack vision, inspiration, planning, or effort, but because they fold when the pressure hits. They quit when it gets uncomfortable. They crumble when things go wrong. Resilience is what turns obstacles into fuel, failures into lessons, and pain into strength.

Success isn't about avoiding failure—it's about refusing to stay down when it comes. Resilient men see setbacks as lessons, not dead ends. They maintain focus on the bigger picture, adapt to change, and regulate their emotions under stress. Each time they rise from adversity, they build confidence and a belief that no obstacle is final.

Resilience is also about perspective. A growth mindset sees challenges as training grounds for improvement, not signs of weakness. Emotional control, social support, and faith in your own abilities strengthen resilience when life gets heavy. Practical tools like mindfulness, stress management, and building strong support networks help keep you grounded.

Resilient men inspire others, too. By their example, they show that endurance and courage outlast fear. In a world full of uncertainty, resilience isn't optional—it's what separates those who fold under pressure from those who thrive.

• • • •

Khari's Setback

By his second semester in trade school, Khari felt the weight of the grind. He was juggling late-night classes, long work shifts, and bills piling up at home.

Then it happened: he failed a midterm exam in his electrical course. He sat in the back of the classroom, staring at the red mark on his paper. Doubt flooded in: "Maybe I'm not smart enough. Maybe I should just quit and get a full-time job. At least then I'd make more money now."

That week, he skipped studying. He skipped class once. He even drafted a text to his grandmother: "I think I'm done with school."

But before he could send it, he saw his sister's sticky note still taped to his mirror: "She's watching. Don't quit."

Khari realized quitting would teach his little sister one thing: that when life gets hard, you fold. He couldn't let that be her example. So he swallowed his pride. He stayed after class, asked his professor for help, and found a study group.

On the next test, he didn't ace it, but he passed. Slowly, his grades improved. Khari's resilience didn't erase the failure—it used the failure as fuel. That moment became proof: he could take a hit and keep moving.

• • • •

Lewis's Midlife Battle

Six months into his new routine, Lewis hit a wall. His weight loss had slowed. Work stress piled up. One week, he skipped workouts, ate fast food three days in a row, and snapped at his kids over small things.

One night, after another long day, he sat in his car in the driveway, staring at the dashboard. He felt like a fraud. He thought, "What's the point? Maybe I'll never change. Maybe this is just who I am now."

But as he sat there, his phone buzzed. A text from his daughter: "Dad, are we still doing movie night?"

Lewis felt the sting. He realized his kids didn't care about his slip-ups—they cared about his presence. He couldn't let one bad week erase his commitment.

The next morning, he reset. He laced up his sneakers and went for a walk—not a sprint, not a marathon, just a walk. He cleaned up his diet meal by meal. He apologized to his kids for being short with them. And then he kept going.

That became Lewis's turning point. Resilience taught him that progress isn't about perfection—it's about recovery. Every time he got back up, he built a new layer of strength.

Why Resilience Matters

Resilience keeps you in the fight when everything else says to quit. Life guarantees struggle. No man escapes it. But resilience is what separates those who get crushed from those who grow stronger.

Here's what resilience does for you:

Turns Setbacks into Lessons – Every failure becomes a stepping stone.

Keeps You Moving – Even when progress feels slow, resilience keeps you in the fight.

Builds Inner Strength – The struggles you survive make you tougher for the next battle.

Shields Your Mind – Resilient men don't let negativity or doubt destroy them.

Inspires Others – When you bounce back, you give others permission to do the same.

10 Practical Ways to Build Resilience

1. Reframe failure
2. Develop emotional control
3. Stay physically strong
4. Lean on mentors
5. Practice gratitude
6. Set small wins
7. Stay connected
8. Rest strategically
9. Adjust your plan
10. Keep perspective

Reflection Questions

- What setback has taught me the most?
- Do I see failure as a dead end or a stepping stone?
- Who supports me when I fall?

Key Takeaways

- Resilience is getting back up.
- Every setback carries a lesson.
- Build strong support systems.

Action Step

Write down three recent challenges or failures. For each, answer:

- What did I learn?
- How can I grow from this?
- What will I do differently next time?

Do this every week. Every fall becomes a step forward. Every struggle becomes a ladder.

Because a man who masters resilience doesn't just survive life—he dominates it.

Conclusion
Living the VIPER Code

• • • •

You've walked through the five principles: Vision, Inspiration, Plan, Effort, and Resilience. But knowing them is not enough.

By embracing these principles, you can navigate the complexities of life and achieve your goals. This code is not just a guide; it is a mindset that empowers you to create the life you envision. By internalizing and applying the VIPER formula, you will be well equipped to turn your aspirations into achievements.

The question is: will you live them?

Two men, two different stages of life—one code:

Khari's VIPER Journey

At 18, Khari could have drifted into the same cycles around him. But instead:

- Vision – He pictured himself in a cap and gown, with a career, his own car, and his own place.
- Inspiration – His little sister's words, "I want to be like you," lit the fire he needed.
- Plan – He mapped his first steps: apply to trade school, save money, and stay consistent.
- Effort – He worked late shifts, studied when tired, and stayed consistent when others gave up.
- Resilience – He failed a test, almost quit, but chose to rise and keep going.

Khari's story proves that even at the starting line of adulthood, the VIPER Code can redirect a man's future.

Lewis's VIPER Journey

At 41, Lewis could have coasted, blaming age or routine. But instead:

- Vision – He reimagined his second half: better health, stronger family ties, and a legacy of leadership.
- Inspiration – His kids became his "why." Their eyes watching him fueled his fire.
- Plan – He created milestones for health, family time, and finances.
- Effort – He showed up daily—5:30 a.m. walks, family dinners, and steady discipline.
- Resilience – When he slipped, he didn't quit. He reset, recovered, and kept moving.

Lewis's story proves that no matter how far you've gone or how old you are, it's never too late to live by a code.

The Universal Code

Khari and Lewis are different in age, background, and circumstance. But what unites them is the code.

- Vision gave them direction.
- Inspiration gave them fire.
- Planning gave them a bridge.
- Effort gave them progress.
- Resilience gave them endurance.

That same code is now in your hands.

The question is: will you activate it?

A man who embodies VIPER moves with purpose. He doesn't drift. He doesn't quit. He doesn't settle for mediocrity. He sees what he wants, fuels his fire, maps his steps, works relentlessly, and rises stronger after every fall.

Apply VIPER daily. Take ownership of your life. Step up, work hard, and rise when life knocks you down.

The greatest battles men face are not outside—they're inside. Fear, doubt, comfort.

The VIPER Creed

I live with vision.
I move with purpose.
I act with discipline.
I rise with resilience.
I build legacy by choice, not by chance.

Worksheet 1: Creating Your Vision

Step 1: Write down where you see yourself in 5 years (career, health, relationships).

____

____

____

Step 2: Clarify why these goals matter to you.

____

____

____

Step 3: Define one 'North Star' statement: 'I am a man who ________.'

____

____

____

Step 4: Collect 2–3 images, quotes, or words that represent your vision.

____

____

____

Step 5: Put your vision somewhere visible and review it weekly.

____

____

____

Worksheet 2: Finding Your Inspiration

Step 1: List three people or moments that inspire you and explain why.

Step 2: Identify the qualities in them that you want to model.

Step 3: Write your top "why" for pursuing your goals.

Step 4: Choose a daily ritual (song, prayer, or quote) that sparks motivation.

____

____

____

Step 5: Remove one negative influence and replace it with a positive one.

____

____

____

Worksheet 3: Building Your Plan

Step 1: Write down one big 12-month goal.

Step 2: Break it into three milestones.

Step 3: List small weekly actions that move you closer.

Step 4: Identify possible roadblocks and create backup plans.

____

____

____

Step 5: Review and adjust your plan every Sunday.

____

____

____

Worksheet 4: Effort Tracker

Step 1: Rate your effort in one key area on a scale of 1–10.

____

____

____

Step 2: Commit to improving your effort in that area by 20%.

____

____

____

Step 3: Track your effort daily for a week (use numbers or short notes).

____

____

____

Step 4: Eliminate one distraction that holds you back.

___

___

___

Step 5: Celebrate your progress at the end of the week.

___

___

___

Worksheet 5: Resilience Builder

Step 1: Write down a past setback and what it taught you.

____

____

____

Step 2: Reframe it as growth, not failure.

____

____

____

Step 3: Identify your biggest challenge right now.

____

____

____

Step 4: Write how you will respond with resilience.

____

____

____

Step 5: List two to three people you can lean on when life gets hard.

____

____

____

Author Bio

Edet (A-det) Martin is a retired U.S. Army veteran with 21 years of service, where he forged resilience, discipline, and leadership in some of the toughest environments on earth. After leaving the military, he dedicated his life to helping men rise with purpose, strength, and clarity. His first book, Man Up: Volume 1, became a wake-up call for men ready to take responsibility for their choices. Now, with Man Up: Volume 2: VIPER: A Winner's Code, Martin provides men with a practical framework for building lives of impact through Vision, Inspiration, Plan, Effort, and Resilience.

www.ingramcontent.com/pod-product-compliance
Lightning Source LLC
LaVergne TN
LVHW010544100826
845148LV00013B/2590